TALES *of the* UNDERGROUND

TALES *of the* UNDERGROUND

Observations of Madcap Life on London's Transport Network

OLAYEMI KARIM

Tales of the Underground
Observations of Madcap Life on London's Transport Network

Copyright © 2016 Olayemi KARIM.

All rights reserved. No part of this book may be used or reproduced by any means, graphic, electronic, or mechanical, including photocopying, recording, taping or by any information storage retrieval system without the written permission of the author except in the case of brief quotations embodied in critical articles and reviews.

iUniverse books may be ordered through booksellers or by contacting:

iUniverse
1663 Liberty Drive
Bloomington, IN 47403
www.iuniverse.com
1-800-Authors (1-800-288-4677)

Because of the dynamic nature of the Internet, any web addresses or links contained in this book may have changed since publication and may no longer be valid. The views expressed in this work are solely those of the author and do not necessarily reflect the views of the publisher, and the publisher hereby disclaims any responsibility for them.

Any people depicted in stock imagery provided by Thinkstock are models, and such images are being used for illustrative purposes only. Certain stock imagery © Thinkstock.

ISBN: 978-1-4917-9058-8 (sc)
ISBN: 978-1-4917-9057-1 (e)

Library of Congress Control Number: 2016904214

Print information available on the last page.

iUniverse rev. date: 03/31/2016

CONTENTS

Dedication vii

Acknowledgement ix

Foreword xiii

Introduction xv

Chapter 1: Heads Buried 1

Chapter 2: Underground Sounds 9

Chapter 3: Rules of the Game 17

Chapter 4: Private Things 37

Chapter 5: Kindness Underground 45

Chapter 6: Animals on Board 51

Chapter 7: Connections 57

Chapter 8: Oddballs 65

Chapter 9: Overground this Time 71

Epilogue 79

References 81

DEDICATION

I dedicate this book to my husband Fatai Karim, whose prank opened my eyes to see the attractions on the daily commute, the basis for this book.

ACKNOWLEDGEMENT

First, I would like to thank God for the inspiration to weave a book together out of mundane, everyday events observed on the underground. At first it seemed daunting, but ideas kept coming and God lined up different people along to way to encourage, challenge, and even provide content as I started writing.

I cannot do enough justice in mentioning all who have contributed to this book. I will only mention a few and hope that those who are not mentioned will forgive me.

Thanks to Dr Sola Fola-Alade who was the first to make me realise that I had books in me. I was previously content with my regular, but brief Facebook updates until he helped point me in the direction of writing books instead. Thanks also to his wife, Pastor Bimbo Fola-Alade, for her invaluable advice when I asked for tips on writing a book. She said, "Just start writing!" I imagined her silently rolling her eyes upwards when she said that.

Thanks goes to Dorothea Gbemudu-Otite, a former school mate, who challenged me after reading my random posts on Facebook to write a book. She also gave me a deadline, which I accepted without knowing what the structure of the book would be like. I would also like to thank Annabel Kuku, another former school mate who "christened" this book after I accepted the challenge. She said, "We should call this series, "Tales of the Underground"! And so, "#talesoftheunderground" was born. She also contributed a few stories herself.

Along the journey, I had two "big" brothers who mentored me in many ways. Olawale Alabi and Stephen Allen, thanks for your insight, prayers and frank criticism of the raw manuscript. Your contribution goes beyond this book and I have indeed benefited on a wider scale than I can begin to mention here.

I have to mention a dear colleague, Sonal Varsani, who on hearing the idea about the book, caught the vision and was equally passionate about it. She actively searched for stories while on her daily commute and contributed a few to those written in this book. Many times when I refer to a colleague in the book, I actually mean Sonal. Specifically, she was the inspiration behind the chapter on "Oddballs". After several conversations, we agreed that a chapter on Oddballs was indeed necessary.

Speaking of colleagues, thanks also to my dinner buddies Mayu Reynolds and Rebecca Vagg. At our dinners every few months or so, we each had to give progress reports on our latest projects. That kept me focused so I'd have some progress to update on at the next dinner.

Another person who kept me accountable is a friend, Mrs Olabiyi Adewunmi. She once asked me how I was getting on with the book and I replied that I was almost done. She was not buying that line and said, "You said that the last time." She was the first person that came to mind when the manuscript was completed.

Going back to my roots, I would like to thank my real big brothers, Dele Olowu, the late Terry Olowu and Oti Ikomi, for stepping in and being the Dads I needed after losing my Dad at the tender age of 15. My brother Dele, a veteran journalist, also gave me a job in his office the same year my Dad died and got a couple of my articles published in our local newspaper. Little did I know that it was the start of my writing career.

I have dedicated this book to my husband, Fatai Karim, but I continue to thank him for letting me be me and sharing myself in this book. Being the private person he is he would prefer I write this book anonymously. Thanks also to my children, Farid, Arif, and Temisan who inspire me to new levels of excellence as they have produced such excellent results and I dare not drop the high standards they set.

Finally, thanks to my Facebook friends for enjoying my underground posts and repeatedly asking for a book and a blog – both of which appeared like insurmountable mountains at the time. There is now a book which was preceded by a blog. Without you, this book would not have been written. Thank you from the bottom of my heart. I appreciate you all.

FOREWORD

It is amazing how we look and do not see, until knowledge causes an awareness to come upon us, and then our field of vision is 'suddenly' expanded, and we then cannot help ourselves, but to see broadly and take in more of our environment.

Olayemi in Tales of the Underground has written a book that truly opens eyes. Several thousand people travel on the London underground daily, and Life in the London Underground is fully representative of the cosmopolitan nature and the diversity of Life in London.

This book is truly a guide to help people understand the nuances and the cultural peculiarities of travelling in the city. It also records the unspoken rules, and the expected behaviours in the London transport network, for instance, the strange look returned by commuters, when caught staring. You will also see London transportation through the eyes of someone who came to live in London in Adulthood. There are several #talesoftheunderground in the book, and the #14 about the Drunken Lady's dog had me in stitches of laughter.

Olayemi has also explained a number of common sights and thing observed on the Underground - e.g. Busking in the Tube Stations, the Free Newspapers that litter the carriages during the busy periods etc.

Prepare to have at once a humorous and yet serious look at Life in the Underground, and I am certain, that as has happened to me, you will be amazed at all the different idiosyncrasies that you will begin to observe, laugh or cringe at.

Olayemi Karim

Enjoy this brilliant and innovative work, probably as you also commute on the London Underground.

Yemi Odusolu
Lead Pastor, Trinity Chapel UK

INTRODUCTION

My family relocated to the UK in September of 2004, following my husband's work transfer from East Africa. This was also a place where we had transferred to from our home country, Nigeria. I had visited London a few times when we were based in both Nigeria and Tanzania. By the way, to the average Nigerian, *UK* means *London*. Both are interchangeable. So in spite of the fact that I spent a good chunk of my time with a friend up North in Bolton, my holiday was in London.

Relocating to London was a surreal experience. All I knew about the place from my previous visits was shopping. It is a Nigerian thing. Don't ask me why. I wondered what living here would be like. I wondered how I would master getting around the city as the tube map and the tube were confusing. I always collected the latest available tube map and it was more or less a souvenir as I never figured out how to read the map and travel underground on my own. During my previous visits, my hosts always held me by the hand (literally) to navigate the underground. "We're getting off at the next stop," they'd say and I would get ready to hop off on cue. There's so little time before the doors start closing and I was not going to allow any separation from my host. My imagination simply refused to go there and to consider what my options would be if such an event occurred. Do I get off at the next stop and wait to be found or do I retrace my steps back to the station where we were separated? Sigh, the possibilities are endless (also as said in a famous advertisement slogan).

In fact, I was so terrified that on my first visit to London, my friend though based in Bolton had to ask her brother who lived in London to meet me. I was going to arrive at Gatwick Airport. While we were on the phone during the planning stages of the holiday, she said, "When you arrive at Gatwick, take the Gatwick Express to Victoria." That was fair enough and wasn't too bad. Next, she said, "When you get to Victoria, take a train to …" I cut her off there! Sorry no way! Gatwick to Victoria was more than enough for a first timer. She chuckled and asked me to wait on the platform and her brother would pick me up from there. The use of mobile phones (even in the UK) was not so common then. I cannot remember how we agreed train times and which platform he would pick me up from. I suppose as a veteran Londoner, he could work out which train I would arrive on and know the exact platform to check as I was too scared to move an inch from there.

Buses were another matter. They seemed slightly easier to manage on my own after I had settled in for a few days. I would be given specific instructions like "Take Bus so and so from Lewisham, get off at so and so bus stop, etc." Again at the time, we didn't have announcements on the buses, so I'd have to identify a landmark I would use to identify the stop I needed to get off at. I recall one time I got off too soon. I had mixed up the landmarks somehow. I found the nearest phone booth. Yes they used to work but just make sure you have lots of 10p coins to hand. I called my host and he described the bus I'd take to get home.

Little did I know that fast forward some twenty odd years later, I'd be writing a book, a guide to help people understand the nuances of travelling in this great city. This book is not about how to find which bus or train to take, it goes slightly further. It brings to light behaviours that I have noticed in the course of my commute around the underground and overground transport system because a lot of rules and expected behaviours are not written anywhere. For example, when someone hisses at you for stopping in the middle of your tracks while transiting

Tales of the Underground

between stations, you will understand why! Don't take it personally. They are just being the Londoners that they are.

I have taken to writing snippets of my experience on my blog, olayemikarim.com which also started off as intermittent posts on my personal Facebook page.

I invite you to come with me on this journey (pun intended) using the transport network in London and I hope you find this collection of stories helps you as you navigate as a resident of or visitor of this great city.

CHAPTER 1

Heads Buried

The Prank that Started it All!

Previously, my journey to work was pretty bland. I learned to ignore other passengers just like what I came to understand as the standard practice. You know, everyone buries their head in a book, newspaper and now, mobile devices. One day, that changed. I got a seat on the Jubilee line and promptly buried my head in my Metro, particularly when I got to the Sudoku section. I noticed there was a guy sitting beside me and I had the feeling he was looking at me. I didn't pay attention, but at Canary Wharf, he stood up to leave the train and put his hand on my knee, pressing it while he stood up! I looked up in shock and horror at who would have the audacity to do this, only to find that it was my dearest husband! No lie - I had left home a few minutes before him and he had caught up with me waiting to see if I would notice ... After that, I started paying attention to fellow commuters and realised there is a lot of drama and comedy on the daily commute. I think that was the start of #talesoftheunderground.

As said earlier, we relocated to the UK in September of 2004 and I started work the following month, based in London Bridge. That was the start of my numerous underground journeys. At the time, we lived in Isle of Dogs. I'd take the bus from home to Canary Wharf, then the Jubilee Line to London Bridge and later Waterloo, where my client was based.

The first thing I noticed was that many people had earphones on both ears, listening to music. Those were the early days of the iPod. Of course, I didn't have one, so I marvelled at those who did. I wondered how they could hear announcements or any other relevant piece of information with both ears blocked. I said to myself that when I get my own iPod, I would never block both ears. I would use only one because using both implied you didn't want to be disturbed. Truth be told, I noticed that when you approached anyone with both ears blocked asking for directions, they would quickly oblige by taking out one earphone, give you the answer you need and continue on their merry way, appearing to ignore everyone again. I quickly learned though, that the best way to enjoy your music was to use both earphones even if it meant ignoring everyone around you. I also learned that it was actually the way of life - block your ears with your earphones and bury your head in a newspaper or a book. Yes, that's another thing. You must be reading something. If you are not, you tend to stare at other passengers (trust me, there's plenty to stare at) and if your fellow passengers catch you staring, they give you a strange look.

In no time, I had joined the crowd with an iPod, earphones and newspaper or book to go! Back in Lagos, the commute is totally different where we would spend hours in traffic. There are so many street sellers that you can get dinner and do your weekly shopping while in traffic. That's a story for another day, or another book, who knows?

It was this attitude that made it so easy for my husband to play the prank he did. He just proved to me that I had started falling into the mould.

Tales of the Underground

I list below some of the usual tools we use which make us appear like we are ignoring our fellow commuters:

Newspapers

Chief of them all is the Metro which is a free newspaper you can pick up at every train station just before you head down to catch your train. I must say, the Metro is a significant landmark or symbol of life in London. In spite of the Metro, there are so many other newspapers sold by newsagents. I honestly don't know if the news agents or the publishers of other newspapers make enough money. I suppose they do, since they have been around for a long time and are still around. However, I just heard that publication of the Independent Newspapers is planned to end in March 2016 changing to a digitally focussed business.

Back to the Metro, it contains enough to keep you going throughout your train journey with the latest newsworthy events, show biz stories and the associated celebrities, gossip, business, politics, sports and all the typical things you would expect in a newspaper - all for free. It's funny how the celebrity section always has a story about Rihanna. Hardly a day goes by, without the Editors giving us an update about what Rihanna had been up to the night before. I flick through the day's paper as I write and yes, there's a story about Rihanna relaxing by a pool or something and clutching a suspicious cigarette, they say. Once it was Amy Winehouse, she was in the papers almost on a daily basis it seemed. I felt sorry for her every time I read anything about her. She seemed to be heading in one direction, one on which she arrived at one fine day in July 2011. In the course of writing this book, I took a 3 month break from my daily commute. I had fractured my ankle and had to stay home during that period. When I resumed work, I decided to rest the theory and yes, there is Rihanna again in the Celebrity pages - she just released her 8th album!

Olayemi Karim

The highlight for me in the Metro is the letters page. This has evolved over time and it is now called Metro Talk. Readers write in with comments on various topics. There's a section where the topic is freeform. Readers can briefly write (probably 50 words or less) on any topic. The following day, people then respond to that post and this can go on for days. This format started from the then "London Lite" which is a lighter version of the Metro published for your evening journey back home. The London Lite sadly stopped publication on October 27, 2009. The publishers of the Evening Standard, an afternoon paper which was being sold for about 20p at the time, began distributing to commuters for free. There's something about free stuff in this city. There is a lot of value for free, I must say. Anyway, we all know that even if something is free to us, someone has paid a price somewhere.

This comments page was quite interesting in those days of the defunct London Lite. When the paper ceased publication, the Metro then took it on as Metro Talk. It carried on the spirit of the banter we used to get in the London Lite. I said earlier that readers write in on any topic and if it's catchy enough, people respond for days and sometimes weeks until the topic phases out. A couple of stories stand out for me. One was about surfing on the underground. I do not recall how it started but the gist of the topic was to find out for how long and on which line you can stand while travelling without holding on to the rails for dear life. The Central Line which I use regularly was certainly not the winner in case you are wondering. The other topic is related to one where someone wrote in about a couple who used to consistently kiss at a particular time at London Bridge station. This went on for a while until the Metro investigated and unmasked them, publishing a photo and their names as well. Apparently, they kissed goodbye on their way to work every day in the same spot and at the same time!

Books

Apart from newspapers, another great pastime underground is reading books. People read a lot on the underground. Before the advent of eBooks including the Kindle, you could easily tell what the latest book in fashion was. Once, it was The Da Vinci Code. Another time it was the latest instalment of the Harry Potter series and yet another time, Fifty Shades of Grey. Some ladies would boldly put up the book while others stylishly used the Metro to cover it up while reading. Now, your guess is as good as mine as to what people are reading. Technology does have its disadvantages after all.

I once saw a lady reading a book titled, "The New Digital Age". I was surprised that I was seeing this topic in a hardcopy. What was more interesting was what the lady was holding in addition to the book. This led to me posting the following on the talesoftheunderground blog:

#talesoftheunderground #1 – Toothpaste Underground

I was wondering throughout my journey why the lady opposite me was holding a tube of toothpaste underground while reading her book. She finally opened it and voila! It was a highlighter 😨. How many years warranty do you get on this?

Seriously, she had a big tube which looked like a tube of toothpaste and it got my attention. I was puzzled as to whether she planned to brush her teeth while on the go. Yes, I have read in the Metro stories of people filing their nails, cutting their toe nails and even flossing while commuting. I thought I would get my own taste of the unusual that day. It's a good thing she used it while I was still on the journey with her since it was a highlighter after all.

There must be some serious lessons to learn in that book. I wonder how much her bag would have weighed carrying all that stuff like a book, highlighter and other stuff ladies usually carry!

I did not get to see the unusual feat of one brushing their teeth underground, but it did happen in November 2015 as pointed out to me by my contact Olu who works with the London Underground. There is a video evidence of this of a man casually brushing while reading his newspaper. Check this out on https://www.youtube.com/watch?v=xq4M0-nP_cY. Unfortunately, we do not how he rinsed his mouth after brushing.

Tablets

Another great tool commonly found underground, is of the electronic family which come in various guises such as mobile phones, tablets, e-readers, phablets, and the list goes on.

I used to carry hard copy books around. If I was reading a particularly large book, I would read that one at home, usually as a nightcap before bed time. There was literally no space in my bag and my schedule. It was and still is, the Metro in the morning on the way to work and the current book in season in the evening on my way back. Sometimes, it's the other way around though, depending on how I feel that day. Most days, I stick to the plan.

I eventually moved on and got a Kindle. Now I can carry all my books at once. How great is that? So there I was with a personal mobile phone with earphones for listening to music, a work mobile phone, Kindle, make-up bag and other essentials we ladies carry. See Chapter 4 for tales about make-up. I wonder why more ladies don't complain of shoulder pain with all the stuff we carry in our bags. I also write about bags in the same chapter.

With these tools, it's a small wonder that I was oblivious to those around me on my daily commute, well, until my husband's prank brought a change. Now, in spite of these things, I still manage to look up from time to time to enjoy the drama underground. Like one day, as I narrate in the next "tale" below:

#talesoftheunderground #2 – Half Term

It's half term and commuter numbers have reduced. In this season, one is always guaranteed a seat.

Here I am sitting and there's no one standing in the aisles. I notice the guy opposite me. Every time I look up from my paper, my eyes catch his. This is getting uncomfortable. Why doesn't he read a newspaper, a book or something? At least in the absence of all that, people play games on their phones.

He's still staring. I check myself mentally, hair, make-up, yes clothing, all in place. Oh well, I suppose he's just admiring God's wonderful creation; after all I am fearfully and wonderfully made!

Yes, it is the exception rather than the rule to see someone who is not immersed in something while travelling underground. The next chapter contains more discourse on phones and tablets and the British attitude to music.

CHAPTER 2

Underground Sounds

Route Master

Note to self: When on an unfamiliar route, pay attention and don't block your ears with earphones. Oops, I almost missed my stop there!

I joined the headphones crusade within months of starting work here in the UK. At first, I thought it was rude to have both earphones plugged in. How do you hear announcements? How do you know when you get to your station? How do you know when someone is talking to you?

The answer to these questions is that, nobody cares! The aim is to ignore everyone around you anyway. You don't need announcements. You only look up irritated, when the train stops for longer than 30 seconds at a station or if it stops midway in between stations. You frown, take out one earphone, and listen to the driver telling you that there's been a delay. The reasons for the delay vary, but include:

- "A passenger pulled an emergency stop at St. Paul's Station a few stops ahead of you." Now the emergency lever in the train is there for emergencies (you'd expect), such as if a person collapses or something of that nature.

I suspect though that some passengers pull the lever out of curiosity, just to find out if it actually works!
- "Red signal." Believe it or not, I thought the red signal was supposed to make the train stop. Why is this used as an excuse? Would it have been better to tell us why the controllers changed the signal to red rather than using the red signal as an excuse? Either way, it doesn't matter, since the train is stuck and I am late. The reason does not make too much of a difference.
- "Faulty train ahead." Stuff happens, so deal with it! If a train becomes defective, there is absolutely nothing anyone can do. I recall being on a train one day and the lights in the carriage stopped working. The train was actually taken out of service though it was moving perfectly. Another post on Facebook explains my lateness to work on a particular day.

#talesoftheunderground #3 – Faulty Train
Just because the lights in 2 carriages stopped working, they took the entire train out of service. I was in one of the carriages. It was only parts of the carriage that were affected. If this had happened in certain parts of the world, that would be considered to be a perfectly good train service. Boss, in case you are reading this, this is my excuse for coming in late!

- "Snow on the tracks." For this one, you have to be kidding me! Would snow in Europe cause delays? If it was in Africa, I'd understand that one.
- "Extended engineering works." Engineering works on the trains or rail lines are usually carried out on weekends. Sometimes, they never quite finish before the rush hour starts on Monday morning. You can imagine the chaos and confusion this causes, particularly on a Monday morning. Kudos to the rail operators though since it shows that maintenance is a valued activity,

Tales of the Underground

unlike many parts of Africa where maintenance happens years after the infrastructure is installed and they almost become unusable.

- "Delayed service." This happens quite frequently. One train is running late, and like dominoes, it affects all subsequent trains. You can actually get a refund if your train service is delayed for more than 30 minutes. Most people never get around to applying for a refund. I was delayed once where a train was put out of service and I had to take an alternative route in a lower class of service. The delay was over one hour and I applied, got a refund for that leg of the journey and a £100 rail voucher. Thank you Virgin Trains! The only challenge is that I don't have a trip planned in the near future and I can't trade the voucher for cash. On another trip though, I was quite amused one day on hearing an announcement in this next "tale".

#talesoftheunderground #4 – Delayed Service
The train was supposed to arrive at 8:31am. The train arrived at 8:32am and the driver apologises profusely for the delay! What delay? Smh (i.e. scratching my head)

I still do not understand the basis for the announcement, and no one qualified for a refund anyway.

- "Person under the train." I got to understand that "person under the train meant, in most cases, that someone had deliberately jumped in front of the train committing suicide. A Guardian newspaper article[1] in September 2013 tells us that there were 238 suicides in the UK in 2012. While a high percentage of deaths on the train tracks were due to suicide, other causes related to accidents when people were either drunk or youngsters playing "chicken" which is a game where they jump onto the tracks testing their bravery and seeing if they can successfully jump off the tracks while the train approaches.

You may be wondering that since this is supposed to be a light hearted book, then why the depressing talk about suicide or deaths on the tracks? The truth of the matter is that life comes with the full package, with tears and laughter. I struggled with writing this paragraph, and it took me about two weeks to put this together since it is a hard topic to discuss. I felt it is important to write this, as the effects of suicide on family and friends left behind are devastating. So, if you are reading this book by any chance and thinking of committing suicide, please don't. The pain you feel now is small compared to what your family and friends feel when you leave under such tragic circumstances.

Headphones

So back to headphones, they come in different shapes, sizes and colours. With both ears blocked, it's an effort to make any form of conversation with a fellow commuter. It is therefore a perfect way to ignore your fellow commuters. That notwithstanding, when people approach me, usually visitors of the city asking for directions, I politely take off my headphones and give them my undivided attention. I have seen others do the same. People are quite friendly and willing to help when you approach them, most of the time. See Chapter 5 for a discussion on kindness on the underground. I wonder though, about those who use heavy duty headphones like the ones you find on professional DJs. Is the quality of the sound significantly better? Isn't there a risk of damage to the eardrums?

I read on the internet that loud music can cause damage to the ears including problems such as tinnitus and hearing loss.

Tinnitus is a term that describes any sound a person can hear from inside their body rather than from an outside source. Although tinnitus is often described as 'ringing in the ears', several other sounds can be heard including: buzzing, humming, grinding, hissing, whistling, and sizzling. Sometimes, the noise associated with tinnitus beats in tune with a person's pulse.[2]

I personally have had this feeling of my ear being full of water for years, sometimes, hearing my pulse in the same ear. It is not pleasant and it is not a condition I would want to risk having by playing music so loud with heavy duty headphones.

Music

Speaking of music, you could find yourself hearing someone else's music through their headphones and through the noise of the train, which makes you wonder if the person can hear normally afterwards. The strange thing though, is how my fellow commuters can listen to music without dancing. What's the point of listening to good music if you can't at the least tap your feet to the beat? I'd hear this really nice sounding dance track coming from a person's headphones and you look at them. They have a straight face, with no movement whatsoever. Oh, dear!

#talesoftheunderground #5 – Underground Moves

While I was listening to a song on my phone and trying hard not to dance, I saw a guy next to me strumming away furiously on an imaginary set of drums on his knees, in tune with his music. Well, I feel you brother! Dance on!

The song I was listening to which prompted this post was "Lookin Out for Me" by Kirk Franklin. I don't know what track the young man in question was listening to, but his moves looked like he was dancing to my music! It's quite refreshing when you see someone breaking away from the norm. It makes the commute more interesting.

There are some songs on my phone with such beats that make it hard to resist dancing, and tapping my feet, too. The Kirk Franklin one above is one of them. You may not like my choice of music, but what is your "irresistible song"? How do you manage to keep still when your song is playing?

Busking

Another underground sound closely related to music is busking. This is a regular sight for underground users. Musicians register for a license to play at designated spots in each underground station so they enthral you with their brand of music as you walk between stations. It is not uncommon to see tourists stopping to pose for a photograph with them. I assume they are tourists, regular commuters just pass on by. They also have collection bags for passers-by to drop donations. I have on occasion dropped coins a few times but never thought of taking a photograph. Of course I am not a tourist! It may be well worth identifying the talent and taking a few pictures. You never know if they go on to be the next high profile celebrity. I hear Ed Sheeran once busked underground[3]. For more information on how busking works, in case you have talent and need a platform to showcase that talent, check out the London Underground website at http://tfl.gov.uk/corporate/about-tfl/culture-and-heritage/busking#on-this-page-0

Mobile Music Devices

Well, we've talked about headphones and music. These cannot be complete without the actual device people use. First, it

Tales of the Underground

was the iPod. The use of this exploded in 2004 and it seemed like everywhere I looked, someone had an iPod. After trying a number of devices, I settled for an iPhone and joined the mould. It seemed like everyone had one iDevice or the other, or a variant of the newest release.

In addition, there are many apps to go with these devices, that even without a book or newspaper you have enough to keep you occupied throughout your train journey. The next "tale" below was posted on Facebook in October 2013.

#talesoftheunderground #6 – Candy Crush

I complimented a lady sitting beside me on how beautiful her orange iPhone 5c was. She was so engrossed in the Candy Crush game she was playing and she didn't even look up or hear me. I waved my hand in front of her to draw her attention that I was speaking to her, no reaction. It was the lady on the other side that noticed and looked up instead. This has just strengthened my resolve not to be drawn into Candy Crush!!

I had just purchased a blue iPhone 5c and on seeing this lady with her orange coloured one, I was tempted to go change my phone and get the same colour. Of course, until I got off the train, she didn't notice. Such was the concentration on Candy Crush on her brand new iPhone.

Mind the Gap!

A regular phrase you hear while commuting underground is "mind the gap!" The attendants at each station always shout this as passengers get on or off the tube. Oh, by the way, the underground is also called the "tube". This is also announced inside the tube. This warning is so serious and not to be taken for granted. In many stations, there is a large space (gap) between the train and the platform that if you are not careful while stepping on or off you can miss a step and land in between. I have seen it happen. A man got off the train and didn't mind the gap, I saw him slump and fall down. My first thought was that he had a heart attack, but those standing close to him quickly helped him up and that was when I realised that the warning should really be taken seriously.

I must say that the gap on the Central line platform at Bank Underground station is so big I think a special announcement over and above "mind the gap" is needed there. I pass through Bank station most days and this prompted the next post on Facebook:

#talesoftheunderground #7–Mind the Gap!

I think the "mind the gap" warning at Bank station on the underground should be changed to "mind the chasm". One needs to be an athlete to successfully step from the platform to the train.

It turns out, that it was a valid observation. I thought I was thinking randomly. Robin Bextor in his book, The Little Book of The London Underground[4], tells us in the history of the Central Line that at Bank station, the platform curved radically that there was an urgent need for the "Mind the Gap" announcements. Now that we know where the mind the gap announcement originated from, I think there is a need to coin another one especially for the Central Line at Bank station. The gaps in other stations render the "gap" phrase at Bank station, an understatement.

CHAPTER 3

Rules of the Game

Chivalry Underground

I get on the train and a young man is sitting on the first seat. You know, the one where those who are less able to stand have the first pass. Since he is a young man and I am, well, older (ahem), he offers me the seat. I say, alright thanks. And he continues sitting and fiddling with his phone. What part of "alright thanks" can you interpret to mean I don't want the seat?

I do not like sitting in the first seat in the carriage. You see, the sign clearly says above the first seat on either side that it is a priority seat for people who are disabled, pregnant, or less able to stand. The less able to stand category includes the elderly, those who are ill, have a broken limb or anything that prevents you from holding on and falling down on fellow commuters. I have a few grey hairs though, so I just might qualify for the elderly criteria. My hairdresser the other day was so frustrated. She said, "Your grey hairs are so stubborn!" You see, the dye was just not cooperating with her that day after she had left it on longer than the prescribed timing. She says to me, "Next time, you must use jet black hair dye. Nothing else can work for you." Yeah right," I think. "Maybe you are the stubborn party here, not my hair."

Olayemi Karim

Seating Arrangements

I suppose she was right after all. The young man in the opening story was sitting in the first seat when I got on, but I was not quick to answer so he probably thought I didn't really need the seat. I don't like sitting on that seat because I find if anyone gets on, I have to assess if they fit into the priority seat criteria and then offer my seat to them. It's best to sit where there's no stress and enjoy the journey.

#talesoftheunderground #8– Preferred Seating

Two consecutive days I have had two gentlemen offer me their seats on the train. Dare I believe that I am highly favoured or are the greys in my hair increasing?

Yes, I do get offered that seat from time to time, and yes I take it. The grey hairs have proved useful in the end. But then how do you know who to offer your seat to if you do not fall into the aged, pregnant or disabled category? It's tricky but here are a few pointers.

The Aged

Apart from a few grey hairs, in many cases, it is evident who is elderly. I'm sure I have offered my seat to people younger than myself because I may have judged wrongly that they are older. Being on the other side of the age scale makes it a bit challenging to identify the older generation, but I now offer my seat to only those who are apparently older and look unable to stand properly. This is at the risk of looking bad, but then, who cares what people think?

Tales of the Underground

Ladies First

It's not written, but the silent rule is that a lady gets the first pass for any seat if one becomes available. I use this to the fullest. When a seat becomes available and it's between me and a gentleman to sit down, I look at him to be sure that he expressly gives me the go-ahead to be seated. I know I have first pass if we go by the silent rule, but I check anyway. A man could be feeling unwell and need the seat more than I do. But because I have the age advantage in addition to the female one, I end up sitting. Checking with the man is usually half-hearted as deep down I know I'll get the seat. There was one occasion though when I was standing next to a seat that had just become vacant. A man from the other end of the carriage dashed all the way and beat me to it. He must have been very tired and must have been an out-of-towner. The looks the other commuters gave him didn't seem to make any difference. He was just unaware.

Pregnant Women

You have to give up the seat (or any seat for that matter) to a pregnant woman. The only problem is, how do you know if a lady is pregnant? Again, I once gave up my seat to a lady and she angrily declined. Don't blame me if you are overweight. I'm just being nice, I thought to myself. To help in such instances, particularly in the early stages of pregnancy, London Underground provides a baby on board badge for free. Ladies put this on visibly so that anyone sitting in the priority seat can know that it's time to give it up.

Young Children

I honestly don't know the rule on this one. But from what I see, people would give up their seats for people with young children. Most times, these kids are excited to be travelling on the train and rather prefer to experience standing and mastering the skill of holding on to the rails. It does save me the trouble of offering my seat to them. If I had a chance though, I wouldn't offer my seat, their legs are stronger and they need to develop the muscles on their bones!

The Infirm

How do you know someone is ill and unable to stand? You don't, unless they faint at your feet or something like that. I mentioned earlier that I was off work for a few months after I fractured my ankle. Going back to work on a phased return I would head out after the rush hour to ensure I sat comfortably. There is technically no rush hour on the return journey, as it is always busy. Having either a crutch or the hospital protective boot did work wonders though. I always got a seat no matter how crowded the carriage was. It was like parting the Red Sea. By the time I could do without the walking aids, I was tempted to keep on using the crutch. The choice between getting a seat and cramping my style was a tough one, but I eventually gave up the crutch.

In all other cases, use your discretion whether or not to offer your seat to someone else. At the end of the day, if you are tired, you qualify for the "less able to stand" category.

Pet Peeves

Some rules are spoken and some are not. Here I write about my pet peeves, some so annoying that I think there is a rule about them. It's just that these have not been written, well, until now.

Inconsiderate Behaviour

It's usually crowded during the rush hour, both morning and evening, so, it makes sense to be considerate of fellow commuters. One of the things I find irritating is when someone hugs or leans on the pole in the middle of the carriage. Now, if you are standing and it is crowded, I would have thought that the most sensible thing would be to hold on to the pole. I find some people now take the pole and the immediate area as their personal property. They lean against it with their entire back on the pole and you have nothing to hold onto. Some literally hug and lean into the pole. I wonder why? I simply go and hold making contact with their body and they immediately jump away. Some are more thick–skinned. They don't take a hint. In such cases, I say "excuse me" loudly. I don't like drawing attention to myself especially when in conflict situations, but it is necessary on occasion. Most times, there is a quick compliance and maybe an apology and you're good to go. It does help to speak up.

#talesoftheunderground #9 – Crossed Legs

Yesterday it was a lady, tonight a man. Sitting in the first seat he crosses his legs. The leg on top has his shoe off halfway and he was swinging it inside the train. I get on and wait, thinking he would have enough sense to stop while I pass. He ignores me and continues swinging his leg apparently pretending to read his paper. Since I'm so gentle (butter won't melt in my mouth you know) I wriggle around and get to a seat trying to give him a stern look. ... He's still engrossed in his paper. By the time I sit down, he thinks I'm done staring at him and sneaks a look at me. Naughty boy! I continue to give him my stern look. Minutes later, his shoe is almost falling off. The man opposite him tells him and he then corrects it. Kudos to him, maybe I should have said something, but then butter can't melt in my mouth!

Olayemi Karim

Blocked Passage

A friend tells me that one of her pet peeves is when people block the passage ways as they get on and the rest of the carriage is free. It can be annoying doing that. You prevent people from getting on the train altogether. It doesn't make sense then if there is space inside the carriage and people are unable to get on because the carriages are full then, does it? I am guilty of that sometimes though. If I get on the train and have only one stop to go, why should I go way into the middle? I'd struggle to get off at the next stop, won't I? Also, I frequently carry my trolley case with my lap top. How do I navigate into the aisles when the train is crowded? That's a tough one there, and I do not know the answer.

Speaking of trolley case, another reason to block the passage comes to mind. If you are carrying a back pack, the considerate thing to do would be to take it off once on the crowded train, but that doesn't always happen. I guess not everyone thinks like that. Some leave their back packs on their backs, occupying even more space.

Personal Hygiene

What about personal hygiene on the train? In the summer, the common problem you find is being next to someone who hasn't had a shower. That can be controlled though. Take a shower every day! During the winter season, it is quite difficult to be considerate on the train. How do you control a cough, sneeze, or other involuntary body reaction of nature?

#talesoftheunderground #10 – Flu Matters

I bring out my tissue and have a good blow into it to clear my nose. Someone in my carriage is giving me a funny look.

Tales of the Underground

Is she alright? Everything is contained inside the tissue isn't it? Happy Friday!

Oh well, we can't all be saints now, can we? Generally we should be mindful of our fellow commuters. For example, the fact that you like that perfume doesn't mean you should bathe in it. A friend has just written to me moaning about a guy on her carriage who apparently took a bath in a bowl of cologne. She is on her way to the hospital for a previously scheduled appointment and now her stomach is churning. I hope she doesn't develop new symptoms by the time she gets to the hospital.

Feet on the Seats

You don't find this often underground especially during rush hour. It is more prevalent on the overground trains where the seats are arranged differently and feel cosier than those on the underground. There, you get two or three seats opposite another set of two or three seats.

#talesoftheunderground #11 – Dirty Seats

This guy gets into the train carriage and because it's almost empty, stretches his legs out on the adjoining seats, reading his newspaper. My friend, if you want to relax on your commute, buy a limo. No wonder the seats on the Bakerloo line are so dirty.

I have seen the train attendants ask people to move their feet from the seats which means that it is not an unspoken rule. In fact it is common sense.

Olayemi Karim

Loud Conversations

For someone who comes from Nigeria where we converse in such loud tones that a foreigner observing us could think we were having an argument, I get irritated when two people have a conversation at the top of their voices in the carriage. I don't understand why I feel that way, but I suspect that it may have something to do with "When in Rome, do as the Romans do."

One day after work I was chatting with my children and some of their friends. They were spread around the house. One was in the kitchen, another was in the living room, and my daughter was standing in front of me on the staircase. I was trying to talk to them all at the same time, asking if they had eaten and what had they done with their day, etc. Of course your guess is as good as mine as to what they had been up to all day. They may have played games, watched TV, hopefully read something including completing extended homework or school course work. My daughter promptly points out to me that I was shouting! Me, shout? I was in my house so the rules about loud conversations do not apply here! Somehow, in my head, the rules against having loud conversations apply only when commuting underground.

In the course of writing this book, some friends have become #talesoftheunderground correspondents. Here is a tale from one of them as posted on Facebook.

#talesoftheunderground #12 – How Many Likes?

What is happening to the English Language? I was sitting next to a young lady on the train and this is all I can hear "n she like had this accident, n she like crashed into a tree and it was like a Polo. When ... like had her driving test and the doctor like gave her these pills - Bebops or something. And

Tales of the Underground

it's like they don't do anything for your reaction like, but they like make you calm." How many "likes" have you counted?

I think teenage talk is incomplete without several "likes". I read a reader posted comment in the Metro about a conversation she overheard on the train. She writes:

"A teenage girl on the train from Putney to Richmond, talking to her friend, said this gem: 'And like my mum like came into my room and I like literally died.'"

Seriously, if you are having a conversation while in the tube, remember you might be entertaining your fellow commuters.

Eating, Drinking, and Smoking

Eating

People eat while commuting all the time. Most times though, it is limited to the odd sandwich, crisps or chocolate. Occasionally however, it is not uncommon to find someone having a full blown meal while commuting underground. I have not seen much of that, but I recently heard of a lady eating a full Nigerian meal which was a sort of dough with mashed potato-like texture (locally known as "amala"), usually eaten - more like devoured- with a pepper stew while in the tube one day. Someone took a picture of her and in these days of smart phones combined with social media, the picture went viral online[5]. To put it in context, it is similar to eating a roast dinner while commuting.

There is no rule on eating underground. But if hungry, wouldn't you be better off having a snack while commuting and finding a park bench in a corner area to have your meal if you must do so on the go?

Olayemi Karim

Drinking

The morning commute is fraught with people holding Starbucks or other similar coffee provider's cup of coffee while travelling. The only rule I recall in respect to drinking is that drinking alcoholic beverages is not allowed underground. This was not always so, but to control drunkenness and the associated petty crimes in the tube, the London Mayor Boris Johnson, introduced the ban in 2008[6].

While there is no direct policing of drinking alcoholic beverages underground, I have seen a marked change in consumption of alcohol while commuting since the ban was introduced. It's a bit difficult to tell what is in those coffee mugs though, but somehow the ban appears to be somewhat effective. However, drunks and the associated behaviours are still fairly common place, albeit late at night. Olu of the London Underground chuckles as he recalls the spectacle that he and his colleagues see such as, people looking smart early in the evening and when returning home much later, look the worse for wear holding their shoes in their hands. Drunken passengers he says, are common sights daily especially late at night. Many of them pass out in the carriages and after all effort to wake them up fails, they use a trick to wake them up - pinch their ears gently. That always works, though sometimes, the individual refuses to leave the train and the staff have to call in the British Transport Police to escort them off.

Going home late one night, I noticed this smartly dressed lady sitting opposite me, fidgeting. Next thing, she turns to the side and throws up in the carriage, wipes her mouth and calmly steps off the train at the next stop. I got off at the same stop and from the way she walked, gathered she was actually drunk. Kudos to the cleaners who work on the underground! You cannot pay me enough to clean up other peoples' vomit.

#talesoftheunderground #13 – Drunk in the Morning

A guy comes to sit opposite me on the train. He is loud, smelling of alcohol at 10 in the morning, and asks me to help bring out his ticket from his inner jacket pocket because he has a bad hand. I obliged, because indeed he had a prosthetic hand. Following my mono syllabic answers to his chit chat, he starts having a conversation with the lady in the row behind me because I was not as responsive to his chit chat as he would like. He then moves to the seat beside the lady saying he doesn't want to disturb me, I'm too serious. I'm on my way to work. Why shouldn't I be serious?

Fortunately, I have not encountered an aggressively drunk person underground and I pray it remains the case, though I had a close encounter once.

#talesoftheunderground #14 – Drunk Lady's Dog

Crazy drunk lady gets in the carriage with a massive dog. The dog freely moves around the carriage even almost climbing on me. All she can do is scream at him and when he doesn't respond to her command, she drops the leash on the floor in frustration time and time again. I try to get off at the next station but the dog blocked the doors so no one can get off, including those who actually needed to get off at that stop. By the time he responds to her squeaks, the train is ready to take off. Some people miss their stop. By the next stop, the dog has finally obeyed and is seated quietly next to her. I get off and guess what? She gets off the train with her dog! I had to get back on and it was now obvious to the other passengers that I was running away from her … … No shame, he who fights and runs away, lives to fight another day.

Olayemi Karim

Smoking

Smoking is banned in every public place in the UK. Prior to 2007, smoking was allowed in pubs, restaurants and other enclosed public places, but never on the underground. I saw one young man brazenly smoking on the tube one day. Everyone was horrified, but no one said anything. He looked high on something and was in the company of a couple other young men. They were loud and appeared to belong to a gang or something similar. There wasn't anyone brave enough to confront him. There is an African proverb that says, "When a chicken chases you in the day time, run. It may have developed teeth overnight." I suppose people didn't want to find out what type of teeth he had developed and whether or not he would bite if confronted. I got off at Canary Wharf station and promptly mentioned the incident to the attendant on the platform hoping that he would radio someone at the next stop. He looked as helpless as I felt and I have no idea what became of the young man.

Taking Pictures

The lady in the amala story above had no idea she was being photographed. What right does anyone have to take your photograph underground? There is obviously no rule on that, but I suspect you can challenge someone who takes your photograph without your permission. How then do you know you are being photographed? This is the million dollar question.

#talesoftheunderground #15 – The Man and his Parrot

I thought I'd seen it all on the tube. I saw a guy with a parrot in the carriage, smiling at it lovingly and kissing it. Just as I was surreptitiously (I'm sure there's a word like that ...)

trying to take a photo, another guy goes to him and asks for a picture, to which he willingly obliges. People, believe me there was a parrot on my train today, I just didn't manage to get a picture and the guy got off before I could try any James Bond tactics.

I once suspected a lady sitting opposite me was taking my picture, simply by the way she positioned her phone. I did a mental check, I wasn't wearing anything unusual. I was sitting properly, nothing out of the ordinary. Since there was nothing that immediately came to mind, there was nothing I could do. It was simply a feeling and unless I reminded her of someone she knew elsewhere, I could not think of any reason why she or anyone for that matter would want to surreptitiously take my photograph.

Walkways and Escalators

There are signs everywhere in the underground to help you as you navigate in between stations while changing from one train service to another. While some are obvious and in your face, there are many others that are not. On the walkways for example, most stations have a sign that says "keep left". If you do not look out for it, you may miss it. However, once you get used to the signs, you realise that they are pretty obvious and begin wondering why fellow commuters do not always obey the simple rule and end up bumping into you.

#talesoftheunderground #16 – Bump Underground

I was walking, minding my business underground and trying to get to the next train, when this lady coming from the other direction passed by me. Because she was swinging her hands while walking, she bumped into my bag, hitting it with such force. I turned around expecting an apology, only to see her shaking her fingers in pain and giving me a very angry look.

I turned back laughing at her and continued on my way. You see, my bag is not one of those fluffy leather bags. It is solid leather, almost as hard as a suitcase. No sympathy there!

So, if someone bumps into you or vice versa, who should apologise?

Similar to walkways, the signs are on the escalators, too. It's just that this time, we are asked to "keep right". Quite confusing, I say, that one says keep left and the other says keep right. I find that the escalator rule is one that easily generates an angry reaction when you don't keep to it. The left, you see, is for those who are in a hurry. Blocking their ability to race past those standing on the right is an irritation which many are not patient with.

#talesoftheunderground #17 – Underground Aggression

So I had a change of route today and had to transit at West Ham station. I noticed that the signs on the walkways said "keep right". That's unlike other stations I mused. The typical rule is to keep left on the walkways and keep right on the escalators. I'm not saying the typical rules make sense though. In the UK, we drive on the left, why can't everything be "keep left" for consistency?

Another anomaly is at Westfield in Stratford. It seems like there are no rules on the escalators. People keep left or right as they fancy. I learnt that the hard way though.

Dearest hubby pointed it out to me that at Westfield in Stratford, it didn't matter where you stood on the escalators. I argued with him knowing that the British are very rules-based. People frown at you when you make a mistake with obvious and not so obvious rules. It's not uncommon to hear a stern or angry "Excuse me!" when you stand on the left on the escalators.

So we get on the escalators and I decide to test his theory. I deliberately stand on the left. Suddenly, I heard a very stern "Excuse me!" behind me. I hurriedly tried to move away, turning around to apologise for being so silly, only to find hubby dearest behind me laughing! It was him, he got me again!

Anyway, back to West Ham. While on the escalators going down, I heard this guy swearing and cussing at a lady on another set of escalators. This blog is too posh for the words he used, so I'm not going to repeat them here. I don't know what she did, but he was mad! He ran down the escalators and waylaid her before she got down. She was with this guy who actually looked smaller in size than the aggressor.

I thought we were going to witness a fight, getting my phone ready to call 999. He has a few words with the lady and her guy and it lasted less than 5 seconds. The next thing you know, he is on his way still cussing and swearing.

What was that all about? Some people are just full of talk, no action! Silly boy!

So I find myself obeying the rules by keeping to the right on the escalators and leaving the left for those who want to hurry by. I tend to leave a lot of space between myself and the person in front as I just need my space. The problem with that is that if someone who was walking on the left suddenly decides they can no longer climb up. They then occupy the space in front of me. Now it's too close for comfort. That is so annoying! Note to self: Do not leave too much space between yourself and the person in front of you when getting on the escalator.

Olayemi Karim

Fights Underground

No story about the underground is complete without mentioning fights or near fights. The tale above is what you will typically find. Tempers are easily flared by the simple mistake of stepping on someone's toe. I always apologise when I do that, which is quite often. One day, a lady almost bit my head off for stepping on her toe, or so I thought. On closer inspection, she was apparently screaming out in pain. I suspect she had on new boots which were probably one or two sizes too small. Seriously, the tube is not the place go when trying out painfully new shoes.

For the most part, a fight usually provides good entertainment. People just watch, while others pretend not to notice, still engrossed in whatever book they are reading or game or movie they are playing on the respective devices.

#talesoftheunderground #18 – Shush, Be Quiet!

Two men beside me are quarrelling. One says, "Don't tell me to shush …" I didn't hear what the other one said in response. Then he replies to him and says, "Because you're deaf that's why!" Should I tell them, "Peace be still?" After all, blessed are the peace makers.

The one telling the other to be quiet was much younger than the other and I suspected the older one was his dad.

A colleague was also involved in an incident on the tube once:

#talesoftheunderground #19 – Paintwork

A colleague told me how she was journeying one day and a lady on the train was calmly painting her nails. She (said colleague) starts coughing, and the lady pays no attention.

Tales of the Underground

She increases the intensity of her cough hoping for some consideration, no luck. She then decides to speak up asking her to stop as it is aggravating her asthma. Lady says, I'm almost done just a few more nails. My colleague is in shock! She says, "Can't you see it is affecting me and others here?" looking at other passengers hoping that they will contribute. Nobody bats an eyelid. Lady continues to paint.

The moral of the story? If you try to start a fight underground, you are on your own!

Yes, that's what happens when there is a fight. Everyone minds their business as long as you don't tread on emotive topics. Check out a video on YouTube. Search for ***"Racist woman on train talking about slaves."*** A Polish lady was having argument with an African man. I suspect he had leaned too close, something that cannot be avoided on a crowded train. By the time the video starts, he had apparently moved away and was seated opposite her but they were arguing. It appears the black guy had overreacted to something she said. True to form, everyone is still doing their own thing, minding their business. The lady keeps talking calmly and the guy looks like he is the aggressor. She keeps asking him, "Why are you shouting like that," or something along those lines. Next she says, "…it's because you guys were slaves …" Oh, dear, all rules are out the door! Everyone joins in the fight and the lady now turns into the aggressor!

Even the non-blacks join in. Yes, you are on your own when you start a fight, but with enough justification, others do join in the action. I guess people are not as unconcerned as it may appear at first. One thing I know is that the British hate injustice and will stand up for what is wrong when necessary.

Olayemi Karim

Overcrowding

Most of the stories or scenarios written in this book come as a result of overcrowding on the tube. In fact, overcrowding is the thread that holds everything together in life underground. It most likely was the cause of the argument between the Polish lady and the African man.

I was in Canary Wharf the other day during rush hour. This was between 5 pm and 5.30 pm. It appears that many of the workers in that area have a good work and life balance, and closing time is between 5 pm and 5.30 pm. The crowd was huge and there were queues at the ticket barriers. You will find similar scenes at Bank, London Bridge and other stations that usually have high traffic during the morning or evening rush hour. At Canary Wharf, I notice that when there is high traffic of people waiting to board the trains, they actually form a queue to get on. Also, there are yellow boxes (road traffic style) drawn on the floor such that passengers getting off the train can pass through without stress. So far, the queues to board the train and avoidance of the yellow boxes have only been observed at Canary Wharf.

At other stations, it is a free-for-all affair. Men tend to obey the ladies first rule or allow older passengers get on first. But in the heat of the rush hour, gentlemen forget their manners and everyone pushes their way through.

When the trains are overcrowded, sometimes you find the trains jerking very sharply to a stop. The train driver would then announce, always sounding very irritated, "PLEASE DO NOT LEAN AGAINST THE DOORS!" Apparently, the emergency stop is activated when people lean heavily against the train doors. I was on an overcrowded train once. The train kept jerking to a halt and the driver repeatedly made his announcement, sounding very annoyed. Finally, he warned us

Tales of the Underground

that if we kept leaning on the doors, he would have to put the train out of service. Of course at the next jerk, he stopped at the next station promptly announcing that the train was no longer in service and everyone should disembark. I didn't know train drivers had such powers. I'm not sure why he was allowed to or empowered to take such a drastic decision. So, the solution to an overcrowded train is to drop off all the passengers and leave them to join the next overcrowded train?

Tube Nightmares

I receive daily emails from a website called London Loves Business. On July 1 2015, they published an article written by Shruti Tripathi on the 7 tube nightmares[8]. Here are highlights from that list with my comments added:

1. *Unbearable Heat:* This was on a day when the mercury reached 34 degrees Celsius. Even as an African, I found it quite hot.
2. *Overcrowding and Tube Delays:* No surprises there, since it's a common theme in this book. The statistics quoted say that tubes are delayed 170 times a year due to overcrowding.
3. *Lost Customer Hours:* How is this estimated, I wonder?
4. *Rise in Sexual Assaults on the Tube:* This is before the planned change to 24 hour tube service in some parts. Ladies, take a cab if you have to travel in the very early hours.
5. *Strike Threats Despite Tube Drivers getting Handsome Pay:* It is hard to sympathise with the tube drivers no matter how valid the justification is. This is one weapon they have wielded too many times. I would have thought that if a method does not work after several tries, is it worth considering another method?

6. *£100m Stuck in unused Oyster Cards:* I checked my account, and there are no refunds due. Sigh!
7. *Finally, the Astonishing Rise in Tube Prices:* Yes, it is astonishing. The cost of travel increases each year. We'll keep paying up because it is, in spite of the challenges, the most efficient way of getting around town. However, Boris (or whoever your successor will be), please help stay the increase.

CHAPTER 4

Private Things

Make-up Rules

I have come to the conclusion that there is a rule book about making up while underground. Extracts of the rules include:

1. *Get a seat on the train. There is no point in applying your make-up while standing. Truth be told, I saw one of the experts standing and applying her make-up.*
2. *Bring out your big make-up bag containing the various make-up paraphernalia.*
3. *Apply foundation vigorously and feverishly for at least 2 stops. Anything less, you are not doing it right.*
4. *Apply face powder with a brush for another one stop. Remember, vigorously and feverishly is the key.*
5. *Apply mascara for at least 3 stops. Use base mascara, then use the other one and then use the top up one. I even saw one lady once using a battery operated mascara with lights, etc. I have no idea what difference it made but anyhoo, apply it.*
6. *Admire yourself in the mirror though after all the effort, I still couldn't tell the difference on the face from when they started.*
7. *I missed that step because I have now arrived at my stop. If anyone knows what the remaining steps are, please add.*

Olayemi Karim

Make-up

What amazes me about ladies who do their full make-up routine while travelling on the tube, is that they all seem to have the same routine. The make-up act used to provide good entertainment for me, but now I don't pay too much attention because they all go about it the same way. When I posted the entry above on Facebook, it generated a lot of comments. Most people seemed to have encountered the same type of individual applying her make-up. How long do you need to apply foundation? Also, it appears the rule book says foundation must be applied vigorously.

I once saw a lady at 9 pm on the overground train from Brighton to London. As soon as she sat down, she brought out her big make-up bag. After going through the routine in the introductory tale, she proceeds to brush her hair and spray on an excessive dose of perfume. That's some party she must have been going to.

Personally, my make-up routine underground is limited to touching up my face powder or lipstick. I can't afford the risk of hurting my eyes when the train lurches suddenly. From comments in the Metrotalk page in the Metro discussed in Chapter 1, some people are tempted to bump into these make-up artists accidentally on purpose.

Sleeping

Another private act often seen underground is sleeping:

#talesoftheunderground #20 - The Art of Sleeping

There is a guy beside me on the train dozing, while standing! That's an amazing skill!

Tales of the Underground

This was an interesting sight. He was so skilled, he didn't even nod. I had to look several times to be sure of what my I saw before posting this tale on Facebook.

If one has to leave home very early or after a hard day's work, it's not surprising that many people fall asleep while commuting. What I find quite intriguing though, is how people (yours truly included) suddenly wake up at the intended stop and get off. We sleep with one ear open I suppose. However, I have overslept and missed my stop a few times. I simply get off at the next stop, cross over and retrace my steps. So, not everyone leaving the train after a nap on the train really left at their intended stop, but it just appears so.

Iain Spragg in his book, London Underground's Strangest Tales[9], describes another downside of sleeping while commuting. Late at night one day, a young woman dozed off beside a guy and in her sleep leaned over and inadvertently began cuddling his arm. A fellow commuter records this and posts the video on YouTube. It attracts many hits including one from the guy's wife who didn't find it funny. He eventually manages to convince her that he was an unwillingly participant in this short film and she was able to see the funny side. Iain concludes with the moral of the story which is not to believe everything you see on YouTube!

Once I was dozing off while on my way home from work. Every time I opened my eyes I'd look at a man who was sitting opposite me and catch him looking at me. At first, I noticed he looked like one of my brothers so I kept looking at him. He probably thought there was some interest there. Sorry to disappoint you, friend, I mused. Then when he was about to get off at his stop which was one stop before mine, he says to me, "Make sure you don't miss your stop." I politely told him thanks and promptly closed my eyes continuing my nap. The next stop was the last stop so there was no chance I'd miss my stop anyway.

I narrated this story to a friend some months later, trying to get his thoughts on why the man would make that kind of comment to me when obviously nothing was going to come out of it. He said that it was a conversation starter, possibly a pick up line just in case I was exiting at his stop. That way, he'd be able to continue having a conversation with me. Oh, dear!

I suppose this nicely ties into the next section, one I'm sure you have been wondering when it would come up given the title of the chapter. Yes, it is all about romance.

Romance Underground

You probably wondered how long it would take to get to this topic after seeing the title of the chapter, didn't you? Well, yes, there is a lot of romance on the underground. Some so advanced, one is tempted to say, "Get a room!"

As reserved as the British are, this is one area where there are no reservations. Couples doing their thing are everywhere, on the platform, on the escalators, on the train, you name it. I know you may be in love, but the tube should not be used for foreplay. Please wait till you get home.

Once, I was on the escalator and there was a man standing so close to me on the next step below. Another man on the opposite escalator kept looking at us and when I made eye contact with him, he gestured kind of asking me if the man and I were together. I gave him my best cold stare turning my face away in disgust. I was so angry at him thinking that, if a black man and a black woman stand close together on the escalator, should that be a natural conclusion that they are a couple? On second thoughts, he may have been asking so as to know what his next move would be when I get off the escalator. Oh, boy! I never thought a romance could be birthed underground, but I have heard of cases where people meet on their daily commute and eventually get married.

A friend told of how she met a gentleman on her commute. One minute she talked about this gentleman she met regularly on the train and the next minute she talked about how they had exchanged a few phone calls and arranged a date. How they exchanged phone numbers in the first place, I have no idea, but truth is that romance does happen underground!

If you are looking for love on your commute, the Metro is also a good source. Save money on dating websites and head for the Metro Talk page which includes a section titled Rush Hour Crush. The header explains its purpose – *"Love (well lust) is all around us, as shown by the messages left by our commuter cupids. Are they talking about you? Don't forget to tell us if you hook up!"*

How does this work? You notice someone you like, but may not want to approach them directly. So you take to the Rush Hour Crush and describe them briefly hoping that the station or route you saw them on, is a regular one for that person. Then you hope that they actually read the section in the paper, recognise themselves and respond to your post. There are so many variables but then a couple did meet through the rush hour crush. The gentleman in question also popped the question through the same medium and she said yes![10]

We're all up for a good romance story, I suppose. I hope the numerous couples I see all over the underground, particularly on a Friday evening, have a happy ending.

#talesoftheunderground #21 - Hold On

A couple got on the train and though there were available seats, they both chose to stand. The gentleman held on to the rails and the lady held on to his arm. Of course, she kept stumbling every time the train jerked but not once did she try to hold on to the rails. I guess she was taking the advice of holding onto your man a bit too literally then. Lady, I know there is competition in the market, but not to worry! No one will steal your man while he's standing next to you!

I notice though that the sight of romancing couples is more prevalent on Friday evenings on the commute back home than any other day. Olu of the London Underground did confirm that my hypothesis was correct. Grab your popcorn, drink, 3D glasses, and take your front row seat on the platform. You can rest assured; you will be entertained on Friday night if you have nothing else planned. The odd sight on a Monday morning on the way to work has been recorded but that's when I feel like telling them, "Get a room!" or "Don't you have a job?" or something that suits the mood when I am still trying to recover from the all too short weekend!

What about the Romance and Drink combination? Sometimes this does not go well. A couple, who had been drinking, had an argument underground. It got so bad that the LU staff had to intervene because the gentleman had become violent. As a result, the British Transport Police was called in and the gentleman was arrested. Yes, the British Transport Police have to be involved when there is violence or threatening behaviour. That is another career path I do not wish to embark on, no matter how rewarding it is.

Fashion

As the seasons change, you begin to wonder if people have access to one another's wardrobes. With each season, you see a lot of commonality in fashion. I know there are seasonal trends, but sometimes, the similarities are so striking one begins to wonder.

Tales of the Underground

#talesoftheunderground #22 – Hem Lines

I believe I did not get the memo about thigh high dresses and skirts. For the ladies I see on my way to and from work, I suspect the memo must have concluded with "the higher the better".

It is obvious that some ladies follow fashion no matter what, because some girls wearing those thigh high dresses and skirts apparently had no business doing so. On second thoughts, if they all complied with my fashion sense, then the underground would not be an interesting place and we would be starved of tales for #talesoftheunderground.

Another commonality in fashion relates to ladies' handbags. Once, most ladies sported the bucket handbags. These bags were so big that you would wonder how much stuff a lady needed to have in order to fill those bags. For some bags, they needed to be full for the manufacturers intended shape to be achieved. I saw small ladies carrying those bags as well, and some of them could easily fit into the bags they were carrying.

#talesoftheunderground #23 – Bag of Choice

It appears that Michael Kors is the bag of choice underground. Hardly a day goes by without seeing a lady sporting a MK bag. I hope I didn't miss the email, smh (scratching my head) here …

Yes, the current fad is Michael Kors. Everywhere you look, someone is sporting a MK bag. These do not come cheap I know, so how come every other lady has one? The average income level must be quite high, I wondered. A friend drew my attention to an article on the Business Insider website[11]. Apparently, they have several brands at different price points with a high-end department-store brand, a middle-market brand, and a brand for discount outlet stores. The Business Insider describes this as the "kiss of death". Surely, they should have known that for a product that is a status symbol, the higher class would frown at lesser mortals who sport the same brand?

#talesoftheunderground #24 – Hair Colour

Why would someone dye their hair electric green? She even has white and green earphones to match.

For this one, I wish I had the courage to take a picture. I see so many different forms of fashion – hairstyles, hair colours, facial and body piercings, tattoos, and the list goes on. The only way to present them is by taking a picture. Words cannot do justice to these sights.

CHAPTER 5

Kindness Underground

The Reluctant Gentleman

I met my sister-in-law at Victoria station. She had arrived from somewhere up North (I really cannot remember where). She had been attending a training session for her law degree. Little did I know she had so many law books in her suitcases. While transiting in between stations, we kept struggling to carry each suitcase up the stairs. One young man promptly offered to help. Before we could say, "legal aid", he had lifted one of the suitcases. Poor guy, he'll probably think twice about being so gentlemanly next time. He didn't offer to help with the second case.

The average Briton is generous, giving to worthy causes including buskers, charity collections at stations or shop tills, charity events, etc. The list goes on. The total annual income generated by 164,097 charities in the UK was £64 billion as reported by the Charity Commission[12] as of September 2014.

Charity Collections

There are various platforms for raising funds for worthy causes. A common sight across many underground stations is staff of various charities with red buckets, raising money donated by commuters. People always give.

A number of charity collections featured prominently in the Metro which is the main source of information in the underground where kindness was demonstrated again and again:

There was a young man (Stephen Sutton) who had cancer and posted his progress on Facebook. He was raising funds for the Teenage Cancer Trust. Once it was recorded that his condition had deteriorated and this generated a lot of sympathy. Not long after, he got better. Now, while the average Briton is generous, some people are more sceptical, to the point of being cruel. Some called him names, saying he was not really ill and was exploiting the generosity of the British population. Sadly, a few days after that, he died. The sympathy that ensued generated more donations to the charity he was promoting than when he was alive. In all, he raised over £3.2 million[13].

Another similar story reported in the Metro noted that a lady (Claire Squires) collapsed and died in the course of running a marathon and the donations as a result of that, increased significantly[14].

Please don't get me wrong. I'm not saying you have to die to raise funds here. The stories above indicate how worthy causes elicit compassion and donations.

In more recent times, after the Nepalese earthquake in May 2015, £19 million was raised in one day! I dare say that this nation is blessed because of their generosity[15].

In advance of Remembrance Day, usually the second Sunday in November, the Royal British Legion raises funds through various campaigns including selling poppies across the country.

Tales of the Underground

You would find the agents with charity collection buckets and selling poppies in many underground stations. From what I observe, many people donate to this cause. The number of people sporting these red poppies on their lapels goes to show how generous people are towards worthy causes.

Busking

I won't say much about busking here. This has been covered in Chapter 2. I mention it here, because people do give charitably to buskers. Some are quite talented while some just provide pure entertainment. Either way, commuters still stop to drop money in their bags or containers which is more proof of kindness underground.

Good Deeds

The underground is full of acts of kindness which came to me as a surprise because initially it appeared everyone was ignoring everyone. It is not unusual to find a gentleman running to help a lady who is struggling with her baby's buggy or a suitcase up or down the stairs while transiting in between stations.

Most times though, it is not too much of a pain for those willing helpers. I always get offers when going up or down the stairs with my trolley case containing just my work lap top and a few bits of paper. Once, I even had one gentleman place a hand on my trolley case without lifting it from my hand while I was going up the stairs one day. To my surprise, it did lighten the load.

In the Metro, there is a Good Deed Feed section in the Metro Talk page. I quite enjoy reading that section. People write in a few short sentences, saying thank you to people, most of the time strangers, who have done something good to help them. Stories range from thanking the staff of a certain hospital for taking care of them during their admission, to thanking someone for finding their phone which they forgot on the train – it can be anything.

#talesoftheunderground #25 – My Good Deed Feed

I owe one gentleman thanks. I never got around to writing a note about him in the Good Deed Feed section. Once I was dashing to get to the station on a rainy day, and the next thing I knew I was flat on my face on the ground. I didn't even see the fall coming, or feel myself slipping. This gentleman was right behind me and within seconds of my fall, was lifting me up! Oh, well, it's not every day you get the pleasure of falling over, so hey gentleman, thank you!

Just in case you want to participate, there are many Good Deed Feeds on various social media sites. I will mention one which is on Twitter. Check out the handle, @GoodDeedFeeds.

Beggars

Beggars are all over the place. You find them underground in between stations, huddled outside stations, walking the streets soliciting for money or walking from carriage to carriage on the trains using one sad story or the other.

Reactions to them are mixed. Opinions on this issue range from the fact that they could be criminals, drug addicts feeding their addiction, or they may even be a breeding ground for forming criminals.

I'm sure most people have had the experience I had where a man or lady comes up to you begging for a pound or two to

Tales of the Underground

buy some food. Of course, he or she looks unkempt and deep down you know the person might just use the money to get his or her next hit. You give the person some change and behold, the next day, you meet the person in the same spot with the same sob story. In fact the third time I saw the same man, he was smoking and wondered how much he had blown up in smoke – literally.

The other thing I find surprising is beggars who own dogs. It still beats me how a beggar can afford to take care of a dog when he can hardly fend for himself. Are people that generous?

Ed Miliband got some flak in the papers not too long ago, for giving money to a beggar[16]. The same article indicated that charities that cater to the homeless discourage giving to beggars and urge people to buy food instead or make a charity donation.

So, the next time you feel like doing a good deed for the homeless or street beggars, you know how to go about it, I believe.

CHAPTER 6

Animals on Board

Macho and All That

After a particularly stressful day at work and towards the end of a stressful week, I'm on my way home at 9.30 pm. I see a tall gentleman smartly dressed in a dark brown suit with darker brown shoes to match.

He's probably 6 ft. tall and I'm wondering where he's going at this hour looking like he just stepped out of his dressing room. This is at a time when all I can think of is how to fast forward time so I can crawl into my bed - only to discover that he is walking a dog. You'd expect a man that tall and all that would be walking an equally tough looking dog only to find that the dog is just slightly bigger than a Chihuahua!

A colleague and I were chatting the other day about our phobia for dogs. Apparently she had been attacked by dogs when she was younger. I had also been attacked by my neighbour's dogs when I lived in Nigeria. One of these dogs was a fierce Alsatian that managed to jump out of confinement when he saw me walk in. I wasn't trespassing, trust me. My host opened the gate for me to walk in and the door to the dog's kennel had not been properly secured.

They say there are some behaviours we do not know exist until faced with a certain situation. I discovered on that day what my behaviour was if I was attacked by a mean, fierce guard dog. I'm still alive to tell the story so it means I did something right that day. I discovered on that day that I could give Usain Bolt a run for his money.

As much as I bravely survived that incident, it did not stop me from developing a healthy respect for dogs. We have an agreement - me and any dog I see, stay on your side and I will stay on my side. So when I see a dog underground which is a common sight, you can imagine how I feel.

Said colleague and I were chatting about it and the question was raised, should I share my space with animals while travelling underground? Most of the animals you see underground are dogs. Come to think of it, I haven't seen anyone taking a cat with them on their commute. Or are they well hidden in their bags, particularly those giant bucket bags mentioned in Chapter 4?

Dogs

Taking care of a dog or any pet for that matter is an expensive venture when you add the purchase of pet food, visits to the vet, daily walks, accessories, to name a few. My daughter has been asking for a pet for years and since I am not able to commit to these things (she couldn't convince me of her commitment either), the answer has been a firm no! I'm sure the couple in the next two tales can attest to the fact that raising a pet is no mean feat.

#talesoftheunderground #26 – Vet Appointment

The first time I saw It, I thought I was dreaming. I saw it again today. It appears this happens on Mondays. On my

way out of London Bridge station, I saw a man pushing a posh buggy. It was a black one with a red interior. Even for one who is no longer interested in child bearing and the accompanying accessories, I admired the buggy. Getting close to him I tried to look at the baby, only to realise it was a white dog! I wonder, do they have a weekly vet appointment on Mondays?

A colleague confirmed she saw the dog in a buggy, giving me the assurance that I was not dreaming. Another confirmation came when I saw the scene again.

#talesoftheunderground #27 – Vet Appointment (again)

I thought this was a Monday thing, but it appears to be a 9.30(ish) thing. I saw the dog in the pram today again at London Bridge, only this time, it was a lady pushing the pram. Somebody please help me explain! I am now getting curious.

For some strange reason, I haven't seen the doggy in a buggy again. Who knows if it was just for a season! If the dog is in a buggy while travelling underground, as unusual as the sight is, it is still better than having a dog that can freely move around, albeit on a leash.

From experience, I know that pets can sometimes behave out of character or can be provoked if they misinterpret certain signals or behaviours from fellow passengers. My colleague, who I mentioned had been attacked by dogs when she was younger, continues to carry a healthy respect for them to this day. She told me of a recent scary encounter underground. She was going up the stairs and saw a lady and her Rottweiler coming down the stairs. Of course, with the history of her previous experience, she attempts to give way, but not before giving the dog a funny look. The owner of the dog sees the look and is offended. The dialogue between them goes like this:

Lady with the dog: It's only a dog.

Colleague: I can see that. I don't like dogs.

Lady with the dog: Well, my dog doesn't like your face.

The dog lets off a low growl. My colleague believes the lady must have given the dog a signal of some sort.

Colleague: He doesn't like yours either! (… stomping off)

Ok, in a country where there are so many dog lovers, saying you don't like dogs may not be very politically correct. Probably, the lady couldn't imagine how on earth someone could dislike dogs. If you don't like dogs, then settle for Chandler's (of Friends fame) tactic and say you are allergic to them!

But then, do I really need to share my space with a dog underground particularly if I am scared, allergic to or do not like dogs? Should we have a pet lovers' carriage? What with overcrowding, I doubt if there is any ready answer to this dilemma.

Other Animals Underground

Cats

I know that there are many cat lovers out there. We just do not see them travel underground. Since cats do not get to travel underground much, a certain cat decides to take things in its hands. The Metro tells the story of a cat named Oyster[17] who stunned commuters sometime in 2013. The story goes to say

Tales of the Underground

that she got on the Victoria Line and promptly grabbed a seat. Coincidentally, a volunteer (Paige Jokovic) at Battersea Dogs and Cats Home was in the same carriage and happened to have an empty cat carrier with her. She explains that she had the cat carrier as she was on her way to pick up her cat from the vets. She managed to coax the cat into the carrier and saved the day!

Parrots

The other sighting of an animal was the parrot mentioned in Chapter 3, see tale #15. I did not manage to get a picture unlike the quick thinking commuter who took a picture of a parrot he saw. It is a different parrot to the one I saw though. The story was featured in the Mail Online of 25 June 2013[18]. A part-time London DJ, Adrian Jeremiah, saw a man calmly riding the tube with a parrot on his shoulder. Though the parrot didn't talk, it proved to be exciting in the carriage and he was quick enough to take a picture for posterity.

Rats

Yes, there are rats underground and no, they do not travel in the carriages in case you are wondering. You find them on the platforms when they venture from their hiding place somewhere on the tracks. The next time you are standing on the platform waiting for your train, take a good look at the train tracks. You might just see one or two of them pottering around. However, make sure you mind the yellow line and don't step over it. You'll probably see more than rats if you step too close to the edge of the platform with the train approaching at such speed.

How do these rats survive not being electrocuted on the tracks? They probably have mastered the underground network knowing where to step and where not to.

Olayemi Karim

In Africa, Nigeria to be precise, rats are not an uncommon sight. That's another reason to have cats as pets by the way. In fact, one of the KPIs for the pet cat to earn their keep should be, "How many rats have you caught today?" So, if you are visiting from that part of the world, the sight of rats underground should not scare you. Maybe that should be a good reason to bring your cats here on holiday with you. Just make sure you have a cat carrier and observe all the rules about bringing in pets from another country.

CHAPTER 7

Connections

Wrong Connection

That moment when you realise you are on the wrong train. ... priceless!

During my years as a tourist of the city of London, I would pick up the tri-fold that contains the underground map at the station each day I travelled underground. Not that I needed it, it was more of a souvenir. My host or hostess would lead me everywhere pointing out the exact platform we needed to get the next train and signifying one stop before we needed to get off.

It was not until we relocated here and I realised that I would have to get around on my own that my mind became open to the possibility that I could actually understand the map and navigate the stations and platforms unaided.

I realised that it was quite easy (trust me). My geography is patchy at best on a good day, so if I tell you the map is easy to follow, then it must be. Each train line is represented by a colour. The colour key at the bottom represents each train line. Each station where that line stops is marked by white dots with the names of the station on each dot. The map is laid out so you clearly know if you are going from a location on the East side to the West or whichever direction you are heading.

In the background, you can see grey and white outlines with numbers on the grey or white outlines. Those numbers tell you which zone each station falls under. Zone 1 is the most expensive to get through and the more zones you cross, the more expensive your journey is. I will not go into the cost of your journey since the most important thing is that you can get from one point to the other easily.

On the fateful day of the introductory tale to this chapter, I was travelling on the overground on an unfamiliar route. The difference between the overground and the underground in terms of connections is that when you take the wrong route underground, you get off at the next stop and face the opposite direction retracing your steps back to the point of error. That is not so easy on the overground. We will discuss the overground more in the next chapter.

#talesoftheunderground #28 – Rush Hour

The platform at Canning Town station was crowded, more than usual. There had been an event at the Excel Exhibition Centre which hosted over 40,000 people and at the end, some of the attendees filled the station. It seemed like everyone wanted to go home at the same time. A train arrives on the platform and it is a mad rush to get on. Not minding the fact that there are hundreds of people on the platform, the doors start to close within a few seconds of letting the passengers out. I suspect there is a 10 second rule the drivers follow: Arrive at the platform, Allow 5 seconds for passengers to get off, Allow another 5 seconds for those waiting to get on, then, "mind the closing doors!". This gentleman must have tried a number of times to get on and being tired of waiting, tries to force his way in, in spite of the doors closing. Now no one would have batted an eye lid, but he had a little girl with him. She could not have been more than 5 years old! Everyone on the platform, including yours truly, screamed out loud. Fortunately, they managed to squeeze in without getting hit by the closing doors.

I suspect the man in the tale above was from out of town. The truth of the matter is, if you miss one train, there is another right behind it waiting to get to the platform, especially during rush hour. There is no need to fret.

Delays

Agreed there is a train arriving at the platform every few minutes. In fact, one of the things I found fascinating as a visitor in those days was the fact that the display would show for example, that the next train would arrive in 2 minutes and as day follows night, two minutes later, there was the train. I didn't know that delays were a common occurrence.

#talesoftheunderground #29 – Follow the Leader

I arrive at the Northern Line platform at Bank to take the train to London Bridge, which is just one stop away. I arrive just in time to hear the announcer saying that trains will not stop at London Bridge due to a fire alert at the station. Just as I'm contemplating my next move, a lady (most likely a visitor to the city) approaches me. She is confused and does not know how to go about her journey. She also was headed in that direction. I assured her that I'm headed that way as well. The prospect of coming out to the surface to take a bus was not appealing. I wait while a few trains come and go, all the while concerned that I now have to lead this lady at a time when I was not sure of my next move. The fourth train arrives and I tell her we are getting on this one. I thought, worst case, we would get off at the stop after London Bridge and take a bus back. As we take off, the driver announces, "Trains are now stopping at London Bridge!" My gamble paid off!

When there are interruptions to your journey, it is easy to quickly look for an alternative route. The idea of being on the move makes you feel like you are making progress, albeit on a longer journey. Husband dearest gave me a tip. When a train is cancelled, or if there is a significant disruption to your journey, just wait. The controllers and all those who are working behind the scenes are most likely running around frantically looking for a way to resolve the problem as soon as possible. The time you spend on your alternative route can best be spent calmly sitting on the platform waiting for the controllers to resolve the issue.

That theory works most of the time, I have come to discover. But sometimes, it's best to count your losses and find an alternative route. The only problem is how do you know when to do this?

For one, when the tube drivers go on strike (this is now becoming a regular occurrence), the alternative is the best option. Use the bus or work from home. As for the strike by tube drivers, I think this is losing its value as it is a weapon they have wielded too often. Even when you are justified, if you make too much noise, you lose credibility.

Interconnections

So back to the tube map, while the map is easy to read and identify your route, it does not always tell the full story and you can only discover this from experience. For example, if you are changing trains between 2 lines at Bank station, the dot

Tales of the Underground

connecting the Northern Line and the Central line may make you think it is an easy transition. This is not so. It is a fairly long walk to get from one platform and then there are the stairs to contend with. Also, you would think that the interconnection between Bank and Monument would be easy, but the reality is something else.

Try the following and see how easy or not so easy it is to do the interchange at these stations:

- Change from Central Line at Bank station to District Line at Monument station
- Change from Jubilee Line at Waterloo to Bakerloo Line at the same station
- Change from Jubilee Line at Canary Wharf to the DLR at the same station
- Get off at Kings Cross St Pancras from the Northern Line and go to St Pancras overground platform
- Change from any underground line at Liverpool Street station to the overground platform

While conducting this experiment, make sure you do not have a specific train to catch. Just do it for the fun of proving me right or wrong. It's not all hard work though. One of my favourite interchanges is between the Central Line and the District Line at Mile End. You literally walk across the platform to the other side. I notice the trains are timed such that as you arrive on the platform on the Central Line, the next District Line train arrives within a minute or two.

Emergency Stop

What do you do if there is an emergency and you really need to get off the train? Fortunately, the distance between stops is not that long, so most times you can wait till the next stop and disembark to tend to your emergency. There is an emergency lever in each carriage if the situation is unbearable and you really need attention. But then there is a penalty for misuse. Besides, if you pull the emergency stop lever, the train will stop, and the driver will slowly inch towards the next stop so you can get the desired attention. It doesn't sound very useful then, this emergency stop lever. This is also a reason that comes up frequently to explain train delays. See Chapter 2.

#talesoftheunderground #30 – Helpful Advice (or not?)

I get on the train and a lady offers me a seat as the carriage was already filling up. I declined politely, noticing that she had two young kids, a boy and a girl, with her. The little girl was standing and the mum had offered me her daughter's seat. I then noticed that the little girl was doubled over, legs crossed and doing a little dance. Yes, she needed to pee. I've seen that move with my kids before and I know there's only one outcome. I advised the lady that her little girl would not last long in that condition. I also asked her where she planned to end her journey. She replied that she intended to stay on until we arrive at her destination which was a station that was about 5 stops away. I say to her, my advice is, get off at the next stop and find the nearest available toilet. The little girl keeps dancing, looking at me. At the next stop she took my advice and left the train much to the relief of the girl. I hope they found a toilet though, as I have no idea if that station has a toilet.

So, if you need a toilet break, would that be enough reason to pull the emergency lever? A friend tells me of a man who needed to go real bad, and this was number 2. She swears it is a true story. Since he couldn't hold it any longer, he gets out a plastic bag and somehow relieves himself. Again, she swears it is a true story, as I cannot imagine how he could pull that off. He does his business and the carriage is now stinking so badly. A

Tales of the Underground

fellow passenger pulls the emergency lever and the train slowly pulls into the next station where the man is arrested. Really, she insists it is a true story. I leave the details to your imagination. He is arrested and given a lifetime ban from taking public transport. Beats me how she knows this part of the story, and how the authorities plan to implement the punishment. But then, she swears it is a true story!

CHAPTER 8

Oddballs

The initial plan for this book did not include this chapter. Thanks to one of my regular contributors to *#talesoftheunderground*, we agreed this is a chapter that can host all the oddities we come across in the underground, which cannot be categorised. The underground really provides entertainment!

Show off - 2 Balls

One day, I was travelling on my way to work and I was fortunate to get a seat. The seat beside me becomes vacant and this gentleman, who had been standing, quickly grabbed the seat. As soon as he sits down, he brings out a set of two softballs. They look like these pressure balls, you know, the type you squeeze when under pressure and to keep you from punching somebody in the face. I'm sure some of you are familiar with those balls. He starts rolling them around his left hand continuously. I must say he was quite skilled at doing that as none of the balls fell down even though he wasn't looking at them. In his right hand, he has a newspaper (the Metro, of course). He keeps rolling both balls in his left hand, while holding the paper and turning the pages awkwardly with his right hand. Talk about attention seeking! I kept sneaking a look to be sure that I understood what exactly he was doing. While he was so good with his left hand, the right hand did not look comfortable in any way. He might as well have kept

Olayemi Karim

only the left hand busy and freed the right hand. As far as I am concerned, he was just showing off.

Height Issues

This very tall gentleman is standing in the crowded aisle while I am sitting down. We get to a stop where many passengers get off and he has some more room. He promptly balances himself properly but facing me. Because of his height, my eyes are directly in front of his crotch area! Thank God for the Metro, I bury my head in the paper until one of us gets off. Good thing, he got off before me. Where was I supposed to look if I didn't have the paper or something to bury my head in?

Used Newspapers

Speaking of the Metro or Evening Standard, I used to pick up discarded newspapers on the train if I missed the fresh pile at the station. I never thought anything of it until I saw a man reading his paper one day. He needed to sneeze and sneezed right into the middle of the page he was reading. When he got to his stop, he dropped the paper on the seat and walked off. So, an unsuspecting commuter could easily pick up the paper and who knows what gets on their hands? Now, if I don't get a fresh one from the station, I abstain, thank you very much.

Bad Manners

Another gentleman was on the train one day. He was reading something. This time it was not the Metro but some printouts. Maybe he was on his way to work. Of course, it was a weekday during rush hour and he was holding these sheets of paper. Where else would he be going? Anyway, he starts digging into his right nostril with one of his fingers. Not satisfied, he changes to one of his left fingers and starts digging into the left nostril. He keeps at it for a few minutes. Good thing I was not standing near him. In fact, the train was so crowded, there wasn't enough space for me to open my newspaper and I could only stare ahead watching this act of his. He was completely oblivious to his surroundings. Ugh!

School Trip

A friend observed three teachers taking some school kids on a school trip. They all got into the carriage and the following dialogue ensues:

Teacher 1 (shouting): I said wait! I need to make sure everyone got on the train. (Meanwhile, the train is already moving). How many have we got?

He counts and gets 7 on his side.

Teacher 1 to Teacher 2: How many have you got?

Teacher 2: I have 5!

Teacher 1: We are missing one. Who didn't get on?

Teacher 2: Ahhh!

They all do a recount.

Teacher 3: We have 13 in all.

Teacher 3: (in local language) See the small short one here? Thank God!

Surely they would have done a count before getting on the train? They were lucky there was no missing kid. I can only imagine what type of future they would have without being able to work for the rest of their lives.

Olayemi Karim

Crying Lady on a Bus

One evening, I got on the bus a bit later than usual, and there were only a few passengers on board. There was a lady, probably in her thirties who sat by herself in the back crying. I was shocked that everyone on the bus seemed unconcerned about her. How come nobody was interested in her case? I walked up to her asking if she was alright. In between sniffles, I gathered she had lost her phone. What happened I asked? She had apparently been shopping and somehow managed to drop her phone.

I was puzzled, not quite sure how to respond. I asked a few questions, she didn't seem to have any answers to the questions I asked her, which in my opinion would have helped her (or us) in retracing her steps and possibly the phone. Or at least, get to a point where she could check with the shop or shops identified, if she left her phone there by any chance. She preferred instead to keep crying and bemoaning her fate.

Fortunately, we got to my stop and I had to excuse myself. No wonder she was crying alone. The people on the bus may have tried to help her and on getting no answers, they decided to ignore her. What was that all about? I wondered. Maybe the next person who gets on after me will be more successful in trying to help her. I gladly got off the bus.

Now the Observed

In the 2 balls story, there were times my curiosity got the better of me and I wasn't satisfied with the few glances to confirm the developing story. I gave up trying to read my newspaper and focused my sideways glance at the gentleman and his antics. I turn around a few minutes later to see that a lady standing nearby had been staring at me. Oh well, I guess I can also

Tales of the Underground

provide entertainment to someone else on their underground journey too!

The truth of the matter is that we are all oddballs and each oddball displays their characteristics on a different day on the underground. John Ortberg captures this in his book aptly titled, *"Everybody's Normal Till You Get to Know Them"*. Read it if you can, as it will help you know that you are not alone after all.

CHAPTER 9

Overground this Time

Elderly Couple

I'm travelling on one of the trains from Euston to Birmingham. I was on my way to a work-related training. The train driver announces the next station which is my desired station. We arrive at the platform and I head for the exit. There's an elderly couple blocking my way. They are struggling to extract their luggage from the luggage compartment. I wait patiently and eventually, they get their suitcases out and make it off the train. As I try to step out, the doors close in on me and the train pulls away from the station. I search frantically for the emergency button, I can't find one! It dawns on me that I have to wait to get to the next stop and trace my steps back. Yes, I learned that day, that when on the overground, head for doors before you get to your stop if you want to get down at your desired stop.

Frankly, I didn't realise that at that time, the rules on the overground were slightly different. I learned it the hard way. When you miss your train on the overground particularly if you are travelling nationally, your next stop may be thirty minutes away. Secondly, when you get to the platform, there could be a thirty minute interval between the trains. Missing your train or stop on the overground is not as painless as when you make the same mistake underground. To cap it all, the platforms are out in the open. God help you if you make such a costly mistake during winter.

It's always funny when I see people pushing the buttons to open the doors when a train arrives at a platform on the underground. It is totally unnecessary as the doors are controlled by the drivers. On the overground however, you don't push the button, the doors do not open and you miss your stop. It makes me wonder why we have those buttons on the underground in the first place.

My trips on the overground trains are usually more long distance nationally, than within the city of London. However, in spite of the longer gaps in between trains, it can be a quicker way to get to your destination, if you know the train schedules.

Cycling

Another effective way of getting around the city is by cycling. Talking to a few seasoned cyclists, you find that they are usually passionate about this medium and look down snottily at us underground users. The primary reason of course, is the fact that they get to breathe fresh air on their commute. I think the exercise they get is a secondary reason, if I am to go by their comments about their preferred mode of transportation.

The current Mayor of London, Boris Johnson, is an enthusiastic cyclist as well. He commissioned the cycle hire scheme now known as Boris Bikes, a scheme that had been the brain child of the former Mayor, Ken Livingstone. In this scheme, there are several docking stations setup around the city. You put in your payment card details, grab a bike from one of the docking stations, go about your business and return the bike to any docking station. This has also contributed to an increased

Tales of the Underground

number of cyclists in the city. It may work out cheaper than taking the tube, who knows? The increased number of users implies there must be some benefits, cost hopefully being one of them.

The behaviour of the cyclists on the roads however, is a different matter. As a pedestrian, I have learned that the fear of cyclists is the beginning of road wisdom. Once, I was almost hit by a cyclist. Okay, I was wrong. I was trying to cross the road before the green man came on. I didn't realise that the cyclist was so close. He almost ran me over, but not before giving me an angry shout for daring to step out while he was approaching. As a matter of fact, they go so fast I sometimes wonder if they have breaks or if it is impossible to slow down when someone steps out in front of them. If all the drivers on the roads drove faster when someone wrongly steps in front of them, I think the cost of car insurance will be even more unaffordable.

Somehow, the cyclists have been on the receiving end instead. As of June 2015, a report was heard of the 8th cyclist in the year to be killed. She was killed by a tipper truck near Bank underground station. This happened only a few days after a report came out that a man had been killed as he cycled home in Harrow North London. The debate continues as to who is at fault, the truck drivers or the cyclists?

An article in February 2015 published by London Loves Business[19] outlines the top 10 cyclist incident hotspots in London between 2009 and 2013 as:

- Elephant and Castle roundabout, 80
- Trafalgar Square, 46
- Waterloo Road roundabout, 45
- Lambeth Bridge/Millbank roundabout, 38
- Upper Tooting Road/Lessingham Avenue, Ansell Road/Derinton Road, 34

- Grove Road/Mile End Road, 32
- Vauxhall Bridge/ Wandsworth Road, 31
- Monument Tube station junction, 29
- Camberwell New Road/Brixton Road, 28
- Camberwell New Road/Kennington Road/Harleyford Street, 28

It's quite sad that we keep hearing of deaths of cyclists when there are so many advantages of cycling. Cyclists, please slow down.

Bus

"My other car is a bus!" was an advertisement campaign slogan used in 2004 to encourage bus travel. This is so true. The Bus network is quite good, though better in some areas than others. Where I live for example, the bus takes so long that I have made some friendships while waiting for the bus. Some have been mentioned in the note below I wrote in 2011 on Facebook, I was pondering about my daily commute.

#talesoftheunderground #31 – My Daily Commute

I'm just pondering about the people I meet on my daily commute to and from work. Interestingly, I feel like I know them after all these years when I don't even know the most basic info about them like their name! I thought I'd write a brief profile on each one. Does anyone have such fellow commuters?

1. Blonde lady at the end of my street: She is always dressed in black or navy blue suit and smart shoes. She even walks her dogs fully dressed for work! We leave home most days around the same time and walk in the same direction to the station. Sometimes we say hello if we make eye contact.

Tales of the Underground

2. Black guy at the top of my street: I also leave home at about the same time he does. He reminds me of one of my brothers and as such I feel like I know him. He always ignores me completely and he never shows any sign that he recognises me from the daily sightings on the way to work.

3. Older blonde lady coming out of the station on my way to work: As soon as she comes out, she reaches for a cigarette. I think I can set my watch going by her routine. I know I'm running late for work when I meet her further away from the station and she is almost finishing her cigarette.

4. Man on the station platform: His beard reminds of the Lion King. Every day, he wears a short sleeve check shirt and carries a check back (the one Nigerians know as G must go bag). I've never seen him in an overcoat even during winter. I wonder where he goes every day carrying the bag. Maybe one day I'll say hello. I saw him looking at me today, he probably recognises me from his daily commute.

5. Indian lady at the bus stop on the way back home from work. We always meet at the bus stop (mostly during the colder season) and take the lazy option by waiting for the bus home. The bus is always late. We are now friends and chat while waiting. When we get on the bus, we sit together and continue chatting. Guess what? It's been a few years now and I don't know her name, neither does she know mine! Should I finally ask for her name or is it too late?

6. Elderly Indian man at the bus stop on the way from work. The Indian lady appears to know him so we all chat when we meet. I don't think he works but somehow we occasionally meet him on the commute. He really likes to talk when you don't feel like. Mostly asking questions like, is that our bus coming? How long since the last bus? Why don't you want to sit down? Basically, he asks questions we don't have answers to!

Enough, and now back to work!!!

As of late 2015 while writing this chapter, some things have evolved. I no longer see the blonde lady with the cigarettes. Maybe she got a job elsewhere. She has been replaced by a man who smokes all the time. Even when the bus is in sight, he quickly lights up a cigarette to take as many puffs as he can before the bus arrives. Once I saw him smoking and he had this bad cough. He would cough heavily like someone almost ready to pass out. When he gets some relief from the cough, he'd take a quick puff of his cigarette, and then he starts coughing, continuing the cycle.

I also had not seen the black guy who lives at the top of my street for some years and I thought he had moved out of the area. However, early 2016, my routine changed back for a few weeks and I started bumping into him on my way to work. Strange how a slight change in routine determines the individuals you encounter.

Now and then, I still see the smartly dressed lady who walks her dogs, so I know she hasn't moved.

As for the man who reminds of the Lion King, I haven't seen him in a while. It must be at least a year now since I last saw him. I hope he is okay.

The Indian lady is still my friend. We still meet at the bus stop though our meetings are not as frequent as they used to be. With the introduction of the Bus Checker app, I know whether or not to hang around waiting for the bus. I'd rather walk than stand around for 15 minutes waiting for the next bus. Hopefully, that would count towards my exercise for the day. The lady and I did meet at the dentist's office one day and I asked for her name. We laughed about the fact that we had chatted for so many years without knowing each other's names. Of course, I've forgotten her name and I can bet she has forgotten mine. We still chat whenever we meet at the bus stop.

As for the elderly Indian man, as above, I hardly meet him at the bus stop. He has aged a bit and his limp appeared to have worsened the last time I saw him. Maybe he doesn't go out as much. I had to keep my distance from him though. He is a very touchy-feely person and always touched when you stood close to him. For crying out loud, we are only Bus Stop friends. He did prompt the next tale though.

#talesoftheunderground #32 – Respectfully Yours

And so I met one if my regular fellow commuters at the Bus Stop today, an elderly Asian man. He stretches his hand out for a hand shake and I shook his hand. Instead of letting go, he tries to kiss my hand. Of course I pulled back! He explains he is trying to show respect and nothing sinister. On which planet is kissing a "young" lady's hand, respect?

EPILOGUE

I hope you have enjoyed reading the different encounters I and a few friends have had on the underground which give a flavour of life in London and the UK. The tales do not end here. Join me on my website, olayemikarim.com and we can continue telling our tales. It doesn't matter where you live since humans and human behaviours are similar irrespective of location. Please share your interesting sightings on the website. I look forward to hearing from you!

REFERENCES

[1] Chapter 2, Suicide underground - http://www.theguardian.com/news/datablog/2013/sep/11/uk-rail-suicides-decade-data
[2] Chapter 2, Tinnitus - http://www.nhs.uk/conditions/Tinnitus/Pages/Introduction.aspx
[3] Chapter 2, Busking - http://www.edsheeran.com/news,ed-sheeran-caught-busking_260.htm
[4] Chapter 2, Mind the Gap – Robin Bextor, The Little Book of The London Underground, Demand Media Limited, 2014, page 88
[5] Chapter 3, Eating - http://www.nairaland.com/2254815/photos-nigerian-woman-spotted-eating
[6] Chapter 3, Drinking - http://news.bbc.co.uk/1/hi/england/london/7429815.stm
[7] Chapter 3, Fights underground - https://www.youtube.com/watch?v=uxTkhG3K99k
[8] Chapter 3, Tube nightmares - http://www.londonlovesbusiness.com/business-news/london-transport/7-tube-nightmares-that-need-to-be-addressed-now/10587.article?utm_source=Sign-Up.to&utm_medium=email&utm_campaign=17719-293366-01%2F07%2F2015+London
[9] Chapter 4, Sleeping – Iain Spragg, London Underground's Strangest Tales Extraordinary but True Stories, Anova Books Company, 2013, page 163.
[10] Chapter 4, Romance underground - http://metro.co.uk/2013/04/19/metros-rush-hour-crush-sparks-marriage-proposal-3653882/
[11] Chapter 4, Fashion - http://uk.businessinsider.com/michael-kors-loses-best-idea-status-2015-4?r=US
[12] Chapter 5, Kindness underground - https://www.gov.uk/government/publications/charity-register-statistics/recent-charity-register-statistics-charity-commission

[13] Chapter 5, Kindness underground - http://www.bbc.co.uk/news/uk-england-27408818
[14] Chapter 5, Kindness underground - http://www.theguardian.com/society/2012/apr/27/claire-squires-samaritans-site-raises-1m
[15] Chapter 5, Kindness underground - He who gives to the poor will not lack, But he who hides his eyes will have many curses, Proverbs 28:27
[16] Chapter 5, Kindness underground - http://www.huffingtonpost.co.uk/2014/11/01/ed-miliband-beggar-pictures_n_6086652.html
[17] Chapter 6, Animals on board - http://metro.co.uk/2013/11/15/cat-on-the-tube-oyster-stuns-commuters-on-victoria-line-train-4188169/
[18] Chapter 6, Animals on Board - http://www.dailymail.co.uk/news/article-2348219/Bizarre-moment-man-spotted-riding-underground-PARROT-shoulder.html
[19] Chapter 9, Cycling - http://m.londonlovesbusiness.com/business-news/london-transport/londons-most-dangerous-cycling-hotspots-revealed-as-tfl-admits-under-spending-road-safety-budget/9837.article?utm_source=Sign-Up.to&utm_medium=email&utm_campaign=17719-274184-Campaign%20-%2025%2F02%2F2015?mobilesite=enabled&utm_source=Sign-Up.to&utm_medium=email&utm_campaign=17719-274184-Campaign%20-%2025/02/2015

Lightning Source UK Ltd.
Milton Keynes UK
UKOW01f0715130416

272136UK00001B/18/P